Spring Valley

Discovering
Cultures

Peru

Sarah De Capua

BENCHMARK BOOKS

MARSHALL CAVENDISH
NEW YORK

With thanks to Peter T. Johnson, Princeton University, for the careful review of this manuscript.

Marshall Cavendish
99 White Plains Road
Tarrytown, New York 10591-9001
www.marshallcavendish.com

Library of Congress Cataloging-in-Publication Data

De Capua, Sarah.
Peru / by Sarah De Capua.
p. cm. — (Discovering cultures)
Includes bibliographical references and index.
ISBN 0-7614-1796-6
1. Peru—Juvenile literature. I. Title. II. Series.
F3408.5.D43 2004
985—dc22   2004006125

Photo Research by Candlepants Incorporated
Cover Photo: Yoshio Tomii/SuperStock

The photographs in this book are used by permission and through the courtesy of; *The Image Works*: Tony Savino, 1; Wesley Bocxe, 11; John Maier Jr., 15; Zbignew Bzdak, 22; Bill Bachmann, 25, back cover; Hinata Haga/HAGA, 37. *SuperStock*: 4, 30, 42 (center); Paul Jonason, 10; Yoshio Tomii, 12, 42 (right); Michele Burgess, 14, 34, 43 (left); Tim Hursley, 20; George Hunter, 24. *Index Stock Imagery*: Fotos and Photos, 6; HIRB, 16, 21; Jacob Halaska, 26; Shirley Vanderbilt, 36. *Corbis*: Michael & Patricia Fogden, 7, 8 (right); Galen Powell, 8 (left); Kevin Schafer, 9; Dave G. Houser, 13; Jim Erickson, 17, 43 (center); Hubert Stadler, 18; Greg Smith/SABA, 19, 43 (right); ASP/Steve Robertson/ZUMA, 28; Reuters, 29; Alison Wright, 31, 35 (both); Yann Arthus-Bertrand, 32; Nevada Wier, 38; Julie de Tribolet/ Le Matin de Lausanne/SYGMA, 44 (top). *Throckmorton Fine Art, New York*: 44 (low). *Peter Robinson/EMPICS Sports Photo Agency*: 45.

Cover: *The Plaza de Armas, Lima, Peru*; Title page: *A Quechua girl*

Map and illustrations by Ian Warpole
Book design by Virginia Pope

Printed in China
1 3 5 6 4 2

Turn the Pages...

Where in the World Is Peru?

Peru is the third-largest country in South America. It borders Ecuador and Colombia to the north. Brazil and Bolivia are on Peru's eastern border. Chile is to the south. The Pacific Ocean lies to the west. The northern tip of Peru lies just 3 miles (5 kilometers) from the *equator*. The country stretches south for 1,225 miles (1, 971 km). It is a little smaller than Alaska.

Peru is made up of three types of land: desert, mountains, and rain forest. The desert is found along Peru's Pacific coast. It is one of the driest areas in the world. Only about 1 cup (.25 liter) of rain falls every two years! Lima, Peru's capital city, lies in the center of the long desert. Two of Peru's other major cities, Trujillo and Chiclayo, are also found in this region.

Along the eastern edge of the desert are the Andes Mountains. The Andes continue

Peru's Andes Mountains

Map of Peru

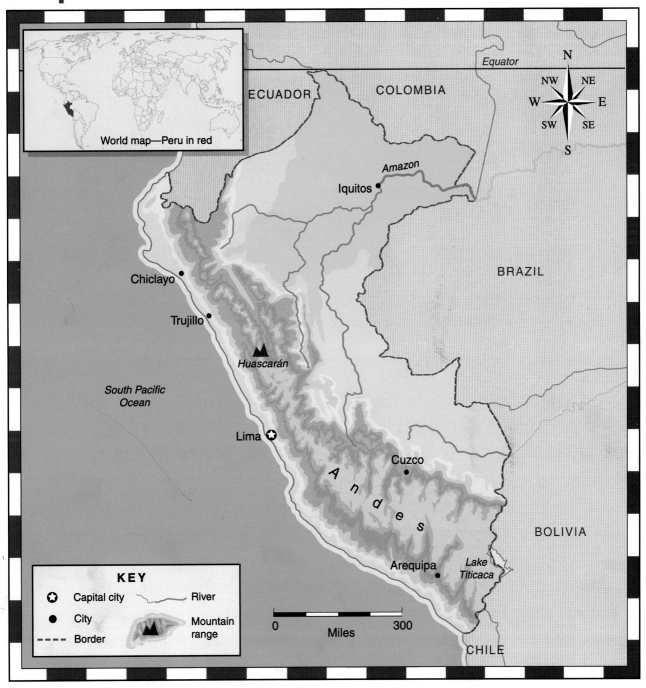

World map—Peru in red

Equator

N
NW   NE
W   E
SW   SE
S

ECUADOR   COLOMBIA

Amazon

Iquitos

BRAZIL

Chiclayo

Trujillo

▲▲
Huascarán

*South Pacific
Ocean*

Lima ✪

Cuzco

*A
n
d
e
s*

BOLIVIA

Arequipa
*Lake
Titicaca*

KEY

✪ Capital city   ～ River

● City   ▲▲ Mountain
range

--- Border

0   300
Miles

CHILE

Lake Titicaca

for 4,500 miles (7,240 km) along the western side of South America. The Peruvian Andes are just one part of this long mountain chain. Some peaks are more than 20,000 feet (6,100 meters) tall. At 22,205 feet (6,768 m), Huascarán is Peru's highest peak.

Between the mountain chains is a high, flat grassland area known as the Puna. Lake Titicaca is found there on the border of Peru and Bolivia. Lake Titicaca lies at 12,500 feet (3,810 m). It is the highest lake in the world that ships can travel across.

East of the Andes lies the tropical rain forest. It covers more of Peru than the desert or the mountains. However, few people live there.

Peru's climate changes from place to place. It has wet and dry seasons. On the coast, where the desert is, there is no wet season. This is because there is not

Vines called lianas grow in the rain forest.

much rainfall. The dry season is from December to April. Temperatures are usually about 85 to 95 degrees Fahrenheit (29 to 35 degrees Celsius). In the mountains, the wet season is from October to April. A large amount of rain falls during this time. The dry season occurs from May until September. Days are warm and nights are cool. There is little rainfall. In the rain forest the wet season begins in January and ends in April. Heavy rains fall, sometimes causing *landslides*. During the dry season, from May to December, rain still falls, but not as often or as heavily.

Many kinds of plants grow in Peru. Some plants can grow in places where there is not much rain. Cactus plants called opuntia and San Pedro grow all year long. They grow flowers between January and March, when it is summer in the *southern hemisphere.*

The Puya raimondii

A plant that grows in the Andes looks like a cactus, but it is related to the pineapple. It is called Puya raimondii. It takes nearly 100 years to grow to full size. It then produces a huge flower-covered spike that can be 30 feet (9 m) high. After the Puya raimondii flowers just once, it dies. Other mountain plants grow close to the ground, out of the cold mountain air.

In the rain forest, plants that do not need to grow in soil are common. These include mosses, vines, and pineapples. Some rain forest areas contain palm trees.

Peru is home to many kinds of animals. Andean condors are the largest flying birds in the world. They have wingspans of up to 10 feet (3 m). Seals, sea lions, and seabirds live along the coast and on small rocky islands offshore. Foxes and small rodents live in the desert. Llamas, alpacas, guanacos, and vicuñas live in the Andes. They are part of a family of animals called lamoids. Toucans, macaws, parrots, and parakeets are a few of the nearly 1,000 kinds of birds that live in the rain forest. Animals including sloths, deer, jaguars, and monkeys are found there.

A blue and yellow macaw

The Vicuña

Vicuñas are the smallest of the lamoids. Full-size vicuñas are about 3 feet (91 centimeters) tall at the shoulder. They have long necks and pointed ears. They have reddish-brown *fiber*, or fur, on their bodies. The fine hair on their chests and stomachs is white. They live about 12,000 feet (3,660 m) high in the mountains. They are small, quick animals that can run very fast.

Vicuña fur has been prized by Peruvians for hundreds of years. Long ago, only rulers and religious leaders were allowed to wear clothing made from vicuña fur. Today, anyone can wear it. At one time, Peruvians hunted so many vicuñas that they nearly died out. The government now protects vicuñas from being hunted. Peruvians are allowed to shear them like sheep to get their fur. Then they are released back into the wild.

What Makes Peru Peruvian?

Before the 1500s, native people thrived in present-day Peru. Among them were the Inca, who developed a great empire beginning in 1438. Native Peruvians were the first to grow food crops such as potatoes, corn, and quinoa. Quinoa is a plant whose seeds are used as food and can be ground into flour. They also developed weaving and fiber-dyeing practices that were considered the best in the world. They created the quipu, a tool with knotted cords attached, that worked as a kind of calculator. The arrival of the Spanish, beginning in 1525, led to the destruction of native Peruvian cultures.

A Peruvian Indian in traditional face paint

Today, the people and the culture of Peru have both Spanish and Indian roots. About forty-five of every one hundred Peruvians are Indians. The largest Indian groups are the Quechua and Aymara. The Quechua live throughout the country, but mostly in the mountains. The Aymara live in southeastern Peru. Indians from about fifty different ethnic groups live in Peru's rain forest.

Thirty-seven of every one hundred people have a mixed *heritage* that is both Spanish and Indian. The rest of the population is European, Asian, or African.

The official languages of Peru are Spanish and Quechua (KECH-wah). Quechua was the language of the Inca. *Descendants* of the Inca and other Indians continue to speak Quechua or Spanish. In some areas, the people speak Aymara.

The country's full name is República del Perú, or the Republic of Peru. Like

A young woman of Spanish and Indian heritage

City Hall in Lima, Peru's capital

the United States, its government is a republic. Also like the United States, the government is made up of three branches: the executive, the legislative, and the judicial. The head of the executive branch is a president elected by the people. However, since 1823, Peru has had forty-four military officers as leaders. Twenty-four of them have been *dictators*. Such problems in Peru's government have weakened the country's democracy.

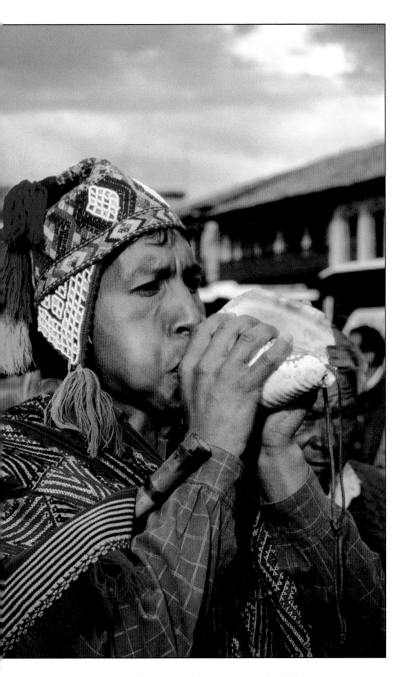

This man is blowing a conch shell horn.

The Spanish language was brought to Peru following Francisco Pizarro's arrival in 1525. In 1532, the Spanish defeated the Inca Empire. Spanish colonists arrived soon after. Along with their language, the Spanish brought with them the Roman Catholic religion. Today, while most Peruvians are Catholic, a few follow Protestantism or Evangelicalism. Some people also practice traditional religions of the Indians.

Music, dance, literature, and art are important to Peruvian culture. Peruvian folk music mixes Spanish and Indian rhythms played with traditional instruments. These include conch shell horns, small guitars called *charangos*, and drums. Peruvian *conjuntos* (musical groups) play traditional instruments, and sing folk songs. Quechua musical groups perform *huaynos*, songs with a mixture of Spanish and Quechua words. *Música criolla* (Creole music) has its roots in Spain and Africa.

Modern Peruvian music is also influenced by Colombian *cumbia* music and American jazz and rap.

Peruvians love to dance. The *marinera* is Peru's national dance. Waltzes and polkas are also popular. Dances to música criolla and salsa are common in coastal communities. Salsa music began in Latin America. It combines the music of rhythm and blues, jazz, and rock. Merengue is also popular in Peru. Merengue is a kind of dance in which one foot is dragged on every step. Traditional dances are performed in mountain and rain forest villages.

Many famous writers have come from Peru. The most famous writer is Mario Vargas Llosa. Other well-known writers include César Vallejo, José María Arguedas, and Alfredo Bryce Echenique.

Traditional Peruvian art is well known. Traditional arts include weaving, pottery, and metalwork. Peruvian cloth and knitted goods made from alpaca, llama, and vicuña fiber and sheep wool are famous throughout the world. Pottery and ceramics are common art forms. Some experts believe Peru's ancient pottery is the finest in the world. Modern pottery includes brightly painted dishes, models of churches, and

Colorful Peruvian cloth

Traditional Peruvian folk dancers perform at a festival.

pieces made for sale to tourists. In metal-work, jewelry and decorations made of gold, silver, and copper are famous throughout the world.

Peruvians are also known for making a kind of religious art called *retablo*. Brought to the Americas by the Spanish, retablo is a small wooden altar with a set of religious figures.

Modern artists well known outside of Peru are painter Fernando de Szyslo and sculptors Joaquín Roca Rey and Víctor Delfín. Other important Peruvian artists are José Carlos Ramos and Alberto Quintanilla.

Peru *exports* products such as coffee, cotton, and silver. The country also sells fish meal. This dried, ground up fish is used to grow crops. Gold is Peru's most important export. The United States is the largest buyer of Peru's exports.

Peruvian pottery is sold throughout the country.

Machu Picchu

Machu Picchu is the remains of an ancient Incan city that lies 7,973 feet (2,430 m) high in the Andes of southern Peru. The name Machu Picchu means "ancient peak" in the local Indian language. Scientists believe Machu Picchu was a government or religious center for the Inca. Machu Picchu features a central plaza, or large open area. The plaza is surrounded by terraces, raised platforms of land with sloping sides used for farming. The stone ruins of Machu Picchu include temples, houses, prisons, palaces, courtyards, and fountains.

The Inca left Machu Picchu sometime before or during the Spanish conquest of Peru. The city was forgotten for almost 500 years. In 1911, Hiram Bingham, a U.S. senator and archae-ologist, found it while searching for another lost city. Today, Machu Picchu is the most popular tourist site in South America. People from all over the world visit Machu Picchu each year.

Living in Peru

For more than 400 years after the arrival of the Spanish, most Peruvians lived in villages. They worked on the large farms of wealthy Spanish landowners. Some Peruvians worked in mines. Others worked in textile shops. The Spanish also brought African slaves to Peru to work in cities and mines and on farms.

In 1820, a man from Argentina named José de San Martín arrived in Peru. He wanted Spain to leave South America. Peruvians, too, wanted to be free of Spanish rule. After a successful attack on the Spanish, San Martín declared Peru's independence on July 28, 1821.

Today, seventy of every one hundred Peruvians live in cities. Some live in apartment buildings. Others live in houses. They work in shops, restaurants, and factories.

Outside the big cities, Peruvians who live in the

An adobe house in the Andes Mountains of Peru

Andes live much the way their relatives did long ago. Many are farmers. They live in small houses made of adobe or stone. Indians in the rain forest live in huts. They hunt animals and fish in the rivers for food.

The most important crop grown in the Andes is the coca plant. Peruvian Indians have grown coca for more than four thousand years. The leaves of this shrub are used in traditional religion and medicine.

In the large cities of Lima, Cuzco, and Arequipa, big-city problems can make life difficult. Many people from the countryside move to these cities seeking work. Often

A busy street in Lima

there are few jobs available. Housing is hard to find. As a result, many city dwellers are very poor. Squatter communities lie outside Peru's cities. People from the countryside who are looking for work live here. The Peruvian government is working to solve these problems. Meanwhile, many Peruvians have left the country in search of a better life. Many have moved to places such as the United States, Argentina, Brazil, and Chile.

Lima, the nation's capital, is home to eight million people. It is the economic, cultural, and political center of Peru. Parts of it look much like a city in North America. Streets are crowded with cars, buses, and taxis. The sidewalks are crowded with people. There are tall buildings, restaurants, hotels,

Lima's modern buildings lit up at night

Foods and spices like these are part of many Peruvian meals.

banks, and museums. There are many outdoor shops and historical sites, too. Sidewalk cafés are popular places for people to gather.

Peruvian food is as different as the country's land and climate. Along the coast, fish and seafood are eaten regularly. Chicken, duck, and goat are also common. The most famous fish dish is *ceviche*. Ceviche is raw fish mixed with lime juice, served with baked yams or corn on the cob.

In the mountains, meals of chicken, llama, beef, and cuy (guinea pig) are common. *Charqui*, similar to beef jerky, is made from llama meat. *Pachamanca* is a traditional way to cook food. In Quechua, pachamanca means "earth pot." It is a meal that is cooked

Hot peppers drying in the sun

in an underground oven. After digging a large hole, wood is placed in the bottom of the pit. The wood is lit and stones are put on the wood to keep the heat in. Beans, potatoes, and ears of corn are put in the pit. Next, pieces of pork, lamb, cuy, and beef wrapped in banana leaves are added. A layer of hot stones is placed on top of the food. The pit is covered with dirt. After about two hours, the food is cooked.

People in the rain forest eat a variety of fruits, vegetables, meat, and fish such as catfish and piranha. Rice and yucca are usually part of each meal.

Ají is used in food throughout Peru. It is made of hot peppers mixed with oil or lemon juice. Ají is added to nearly every Peruvian dish. Peruvians also eat a large amount of quinoa. About 150 different kinds of potatoes are grown in Peru. They are yellow, white, purple, and red. They are eaten with nearly every meal.

Let's Eat!
Leche Asada

Ask an adult to help you prepare this tasty pudding from Peru. Always remember to wash your hands with soap and water before you begin.

Ingredients:

1 14-oz. can sweetened condensed milk

1 12-oz. can evaporated milk

1 cup sugar, divided

1 tablespoon vanilla extract

8 eggs, beaten

1/4 cup water

Preheat oven to 400 degrees Fahrenheit. Mix the condensed milk, evaporated milk, 1/2 cup sugar, vanilla, and eggs in a medium-size bowl. In a saucepan, dissolve 1/2 cup sugar in 1/4 cup of water over medium heat until it becomes syrupy and slightly tan. Pour the mixture from the saucepan into an 8-inch by 8-inch glass baking dish. Pour the milk mixture on top. Fill a second glass dish that is slightly larger than the one containing the ingredients halfway with water. Place the dish containing the ingredients inside the larger dish. Cover the larger dish with foil. Carefully place in oven. Cook for 30 to 45 minutes, or until pudding is completely cooked. (Pudding is cooked when a knife inserted in the center comes out clean, or when the pudding is brown on top and no longer shiny.) Allow to cool completely. Place baking dish in the refrigerator until pudding is slightly chilled. Makes 8 to 10 servings.

School Days

All children in Peru must go to school between the ages of six and twelve. They study reading, math, history, and Spanish. They also learn science, social studies, music, art, and physical education. *Colegio* (secondary school) is for students aged twelve to fifteen. Secondary school is not well attended. Fewer than half of all twelve- to fifteen-year-olds attend secondary school. Many of those who complete secondary school go on to universities. The National Autonomous University of San Marcos, founded in 1551, was the first university in the Americas.

Peru's government is working to make education better for all of the country's children.

Peruvian elementary school students

Students in Peru do not usually wear uniforms, unless they attend a private religious school. They attend classes five days a week, Monday through Friday. The school year starts in late March or early April. Students have a three-month vacation during the summer, which starts in December. The school day begins at about 8:00 A.M. and ends at about 1:00 P.M. In some places there are many students and not enough teachers. As a result, students must attend school in morning and afternoon shifts. Most schools teach classes in Spanish, but some schools in the countryside are taught in the local language.

Today, eighty-nine of one hundred Peruvians can read and write. However, serious educational problems remain. Schools are overcrowded. There are not enough teachers, textbooks, or equipment. In recent years, Peruvians have worked hard to solve these problems. Some parents have chosen to pay for their children to attend private or religious schools. However, many families cannot afford to pay for their children's education.

In the mountains and rain forests, school differs greatly from school in the cities and large towns. In the countryside, children are often needed at home to help with farming and caring for animals. Some homes are located far away from the nearest school, and there is no public transportation. This means many children do not go to school at all.

On special occasions such as holidays, Peruvian schoolchildren participate in ceremonies that honor the country's heroes. Parades take place. Drum and bugle corps and flag bearers also perform.

When they are not in school, students play games or sports, do homework, or just hang out. Some children participate in after-school programs. Baseball and *fútbol* (soccer) are the most popular. Music, dance, and martial arts such as tae kwon do or karate also attract many children. Children in the mountains or the rain forest do household or farm chores after school.

These schoolchildren are dressed up to take part in a holiday parade.

Can You Answer These Riddles?

Schoolchildren in Peru often enjoy trying to outsmart each other with riddles. How many of these can you guess without looking at the answers at the bottom of the page? (The riddles and the answers are in both Spanish and English.)

1. Alquién que duerme en una cama de seda.

2. Patitas de palo con su frazada encima.

3. De día y de noche, camina sin pies.

4. Ese tan pequeñito pero trabajadorcito.

5. Se tumba, se arremanga, se cocina y se come.

6. ¿Qué gusano te molesta en el estómago?

1. This beauty sleeps in a soft silk bed.

2. It has legs as thin as sticks, yet carries a big warm blanket.

3. Day or night, it never walks on feet.

4. He is so small, yet works so hard.

5. You knock him down, then roll up his sleeves before you cook and eat.

6. What bites you inside your stomach?

Las Soluciónes:
1. Mariposa 2. Oveja 3. Culebra 4. Hormiga 5. Choclo 6. El hambre

Answers:
1. Butterfly 2. Sheep 3. Snake 4. Ant 5. Corn on the cob 6. Hunger

27

Just for Fun

Peruvians can participate in nearly any sport or activity. Many different water sports and mountain activities are available. Swimming, sunbathing, and windsurfing are popular on the coast during summertime. Peru's beaches are also excellent sites for surfing. Surfing world championships have been held in Peru. Each year, the village of Huanchaco, on Peru's northern coast, hosts a surfing event for surfers from all over the world. Hiking, skiing, and mountain biking are popular in the mountains.

A professional surfer competes off the coast of Peru.

These fútbol fans painted their faces with the colors of the Peruvian flag to show support for their national team.

Peruvians love bullfighting. Families regularly spend a day together at one of the country's thousands of bullrings. Plaza de Acho, in Lima, is the oldest bullring in the Americas. Peru's *caballos de paso* (stepping horses) also perform there.

People also participate in organized sports such as basketball, tennis, golf, and baseball. Volleyball is the second most popular sport. Peruvian women especially enjoy it. Peru's national women's team often wins tournaments in South America. The team won a silver medal at the summer Olympics in 1988.

By far, however, the most popular sport in Peru is fútbol. Peru has many fútbol teams. Some of the best teams in Lima include Alianza Lima and the Universitario de Deportes. The Peruvian national team plays in tournaments throughout the world.

A busy marketplace in Lima

People in Peru's large cities enjoy going to the movies, shopping, playing games in video arcades, and dining out. Some children enjoy skateboarding. Shopping in Peru includes both indoor and outdoor markets. Some outdoor markets, especially in Lima, attract hundreds of people with items for sale, and thousands of customers. Street merchants called *vendedores ambulantes* can be found in many cities. Shoppers pay street merchants less money for the items they sell than they would have to pay in shops and stores.

Peruvians in some areas enjoy *dar un paseo*. This means to take a walk in the evening, usually through the town plaza. At about 7:00 P.M., the main plaza fills with families, couples, teenagers, and children. They stroll together, or just sit and talk.

Television is popular with many Peruvians. They watch programs

Children watch as their father blows bubbles outside their rain forest home.

from all over South America, and some from the United States and Europe. Favorite TV programs include sports, especially fútbol, and *telenovelas*, or soap operas. In villages where electricity is unavailable or too expensive for homes, TVs are set up in the main plaza. In cities and towns, people who do not have televisions gather outside electronics shops to watch their favorite programs.

Peruvians enjoy spending time with family and friends. No matter what the activity, all members of the family are usually included. This means grandparents,

This famous monkey drawing near Nazca is so big it can be seen only from the air.

aunts, uncles, and cousins join in. In traditional communities, found in the mountains and rain forest, families spend time teaching children about their history, culture, and legends.

Peruvians and tourists explore the country's oldest sites. Throughout Peru are the ruins left by many people who lived long ago. Machu Picchu is the most well known. Other interesting sites include tombs near the village of Sipán and the giant line drawings of animals and shapes in Nazca.

Sapo

Sapo (toad) is a traditional game played in some parts of Peru. In sapo, a toad made of metal sits on top of a box. The box has holes cut into it. Each hole is worth a certain number of points. Players throw metal disks at the sapo. They try to get the disks into the sapo's mouth. This earns the highest number of points. If the disks land in one of the holes, they earn fewer points. After all of the disks have been tossed, the player with the most points wins.

Let's Celebrate!

Because most people in Peru are Catholic, saints' days are important. Each saint in the Roman Catholic Church has a feast day once each year. These feast days are usually celebrated with festivals and parades. In addition, every village, town, or city has a patron saint. A patron saint is a saint who looks after a particular community or group of people. Festivals are held to honor them. These festivals usually last three or four days. Music, food, and dances mark the occasion.

One of the country's many Catholic churches

Children gather to greet Papa Noel.

A Nativity scene in Iquitos, Peru

Christmas celebrations begin on Christmas Eve. Peruvians attend Mass with their families. Children know Santa Claus as Papa Noel. Christmas decorations are a common sight. They often include a Nativity scene. Some scenes feature hills and mountains topped with plastic or ceramic figures. These figures stand for each person or animal present at the birth of Jesus. The scenes usually include llamas. The human figures are dressed in traditional Peruvian clothing. Homes, schools, and office buildings display Nativity scenes. Great pride is taken in producing the best one.

Semana Santa (Easter Holy Week) is one of the most important Catholic holidays in Peru. It lasts for ten days and features performers who act out the death

This religious statue is being carried in a procession during a festival called Corpus Christi.

of Jesus. Each night, people participate in quiet *processions*. Statues on platforms covered with candles are carried around the main plaza and to each church in the community. The Semana Santa celebrations in Ayacucho are the most famous in Peru.

In Cuzco, a festival called the Lord of the Earthquakes takes place on the Monday of Semana Santa. This festival dates back to 1650, when an earthquake seriously damaged many churches. A statue of Jesus was carried through the streets and the *aftershocks* ended. Since then, the statue has been known as the Lord of the Earthquakes. Each year, parades and feasts are held. The statue is carried through the city.

South America's largest religious procession takes place in Lima every October. It is called the Lord of the Miracles. The procession marks another earthquake, which occurred in 1655. The earthquake damaged much of the area. But a wall painting of Jesus' death on the cross survived. After the painting survived another earthquake, it became known as the Lord of the Miracles. It was carried through Lima in a parade every year until 1923. In that year, it was destroyed in a fire. An exact copy was made to replace it. Today, the procession combines Catholic and Indian religious traditions. It draws two million people to Lima each year.

Another important Catholic festival honors Santa Rosa of Lima. In 1671, she became the first saint in the New World.

Other religious holidays in Peru include Saint John the Baptist Day (June 24), Saints Peter and Paul Day (June 29), and All Saints' Day (November 1).

Peru celebrates Independence Day on July 28. On this day in 1821, Peru declared its independence from Spain. Peruvians usually have several days off from work or school for this holiday. They use the time to visit other parts of the country.

Many Peruvians dress up in costumes to celebrate Saints Peter and Paul Day.

Inti Raymi, the Festival of the Sun, takes place each year in June. This festival celebrates the Incan New Year. It is the most important festival to Peru's Indians. During the festival, Quechuas dress in traditional Incan style. They hold large feasts and have parades and dances in their villages and towns. The main ceremony takes

Celebrating the Inti Raymi Festival in Cuzco

place at Sacsayhuamán. There, a man is chosen to play the part of an Inca ruler. He makes an offering to the sun god. Inti Raymi lasts for one week.

In the mountains and the rain forest, traditional rituals and ceremonies mark important tribal events.

Peruvians celebrate their birthdays with a party, cake and candles, and presents. Guests at a child's birthday party might receive two kinds of party favors. These are called *favors recordatorio*, which means souvenirs. The first favor is a goody bag. The second is a pin made in honor of the event. These pins can be so fancy that some children collect them. Children at birthday parties almost always wear paper hats. The child who is celebrating his or her birthday wears a birthday crown.

Make a Birthday Crown

Wear this crown yourself, or make it for a friend. If you make it for someone else, give it to the birthday boy or girl and say, "*¡Feliz Cumpleaños!*" That's Spanish for "Happy Birthday!"

What you need:

yellow or gold construction paper

glue or clear tape

stickers, glitter, craft feathers, tissue paper

scissors

pencil

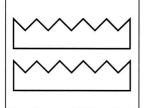

What you do:

1. Draw two crown shapes on the construction paper.

2. Cut out the shapes.

3. Glue or tape the two shapes to form the crown. Make sure it fits around your head.

4. Decorate the crown with stickers, glitter, feathers, tissue paper, or anything else you can think of.

Peru's flag has three vertical stripes of red, white, and red. The national coat of arms is in the center of the white band. The coat of arms features a shield with a vicuña, the cinchona tree, and a yellow horn of plenty spilling out gold coins. These pictures stand for Peru's wildlife, plants, and minerals. Above the coat of arms is a green wreath. Branches of palm and laurel tied at the bottom with a red and white ribbon surround the coat of arms.

The nuevo sol is Peru's form of money. The exchange rate changes often, but in June 2004, 3.4 nuevo sol equaled one U.S. dollar.

Count in Quechua

English	Quechua	Say it like this:
one	juq	JUK
two	iskay	IS-kai
three	kinsa	KIN-sah
four	tawa	TAH-wuh
five	pichq'a	PIS-kah
six	soqta	SOAK-tah
seven	k'anchis	KAN-chis
eight	pusac	POO-sak
nine	isqon	IS-kun
ten	chunka	CHUN-kuh

Glossary

aftershock A minor shock following the main shock of an earthquake.

descendants The children, grandchildren, and so on of a person who lived long ago.

dictators Leaders who have complete control of a country, often ruling it unfairly.

equator The imaginary line around the middle of the Earth.

export To send products to other countries for sale.

fiber Long, threadlike material. Cotton, wool, hemp, and nylon are examples of fiber.

heritage Important traditions handed down from one generation to another.

landslide A sudden slide of earth and rocks down the side of a mountain or a hill.

procession A number of people walking or driving along a route as part of a parade.

southern hemisphere The half of the earth that is south of the equator.

Fast Facts

The desert is found along Peru's Pacific coast. It is one of the driest areas in the world. Only about 1 cup (.25 liter) of rain falls every two years!

Peru is the third-largest country in South America. The northern tip of Peru lies just 3 miles (5 km) from the equator. The country stretches south for 1,225 miles (1, 971 km). It is a little smaller than Alaska.

Along the eastern edge of the desert are the Andes Mountains. Some peaks are more than 20,000 feet (6,100 m) tall. At 22,205 feet (6,768 m), Huascarán is Peru's highest peak.

Lima, Peru's capital city, lies in the center of the long desert. It is home to eight million people.

Peru's flag has three vertical stripes of red, white, and red. The national coat of arms is in the center of the white band. Above the coat of arms is a green wreath. Branches of palm and laurel tied at the bottom with a red and white ribbon surround the coat of arms.

Lake Titicaca is on the border of Peru and Bolivia. Lake Titicaca lies at 12,500 feet (3,810 m). It is the highest lake in the world that ships can travel across.

In Peru, 90 percent of the people are Roman Catholic and 10 percent follow other religions.

The nuevo sol is Peru's form of money. The exchange rate changes often, but in 2004, 3.4 nuevo sol equaled one U.S. dollar.

Machu Picchu is the remains of an ancient Incan city that lies 7,973 feet (2,430 m) high in the Andes of southern Peru. The name Machu Picchu means "ancient peak."

As of July 2004, there were 27,544,305 people living in Peru.

The official languages of Peru are Spanish and Quechua. Quechua was the language of the Inca.

The country's full name is República del Perú, or the Republic of Peru. The government is made up of three branches: the executive, the legislative, and the judicial. The head of the executive branch is a president elected by the people.

43

Proud to Be Peruvian

Susana Baca (1948–)

Born in Chorrillos, outside Lima, Susana Baca is descended from black Africans who were brought to Peru in the 1500s as slaves. As one of the most famous musicians in South America, Baca has performed all over the world. Along with performing, she is dedicated to preserving the history and culture of black Peruvians. She and her husband have founded an institute in Lima for the study of black Peruvian culture. Meanwhile, Baca is becoming increasingly well known outside of South America.

Martín Chambi (1891–1973)

Martín Chambi was a Peruvian Indian who was born in a small village in the Andes. He became a photographer and opened his own studio in Cuzco in 1920. From the 1920s to the 1950s, Chambi recorded Peruvian culture through his photographs. He was among the first photographers to include Peruvian Indian culture in his work. Today, he is considered to be one of the most important photographers of the 1900s. His photographs hang in galleries and art museums throughout the world.

Teofilo "Nene" Cubillas (1949–)

Teofilo "Nene" Cubillas is considered to be Peru's greatest soccer player. He was born in Lima and began playing soccer at a young age. In 1966, when he was sixteen years old, he began playing for Alianza Lima, one of Peru's best-known soccer teams. Cubillas made the national team in 1968. In 1970, he scored five goals in four games in the World Cup tournament. In 1972, he was voted the best soccer player in South America. Cubillas went on to play for European teams, as well as the National American Soccer League. He was a player in the 1978 and 1982 World Cups. He retired in 1986. He now lives in Miami, Florida, where he coaches soccer.

Find Out More

Books

Peru by Leslie Jermyn. Gareth Stevens, Milwaukee, Wisconsin, 1998.

Peru by Marycate O'Sullivan. The Child's World, Inc., Chanhassen, Minnesota, 2001.

Peru: People and Culture by Tammy Everts. Crabtree Publishing, New York, New York, 2003.

Welcome to Peru by Dora Yip and Janet Heisey. Gareth Stevens, Milwaukee, Wisconsin, 2002.

Web Sites*

http://www.imagesoft.net/flags/anthems.html
At this site, you can listen to Peru's national anthem.

http://www.andes.org
Learn more about the Quechua Indians, as well as how to say colors and numbers in Quechua. Includes Spanish.

Video

Full Circle with Michael Palin: Bolivia and Peru. An introduction to everyday life in Peru. Includes details about food, school, games, clothing, and customs. 1999.

*All Internet sites were available and accurate when sent to press.

Index

Page numbers for illustrations are in **boldface.**

About the Author

Sarah De Capua is the author of many books, including nonfiction, biographies, geography, and historical titles. She enjoys traveling and writing books about the places she has visited when she gets home. Born and raised in Connecticut, she now lives in Colorado.

Acknowledgments

My thanks to Rosario Rosenberger of St. Thomas Aquinas Church in Alpharetta, Georgia, for her invaluable assistance. *¡Gracias!*